ABOVE: *The purpose of the spinning wheel is to impart twist on to the fibres being spun and to wind the resulting yarn on to the bobbin. In the type of wheel illustrated a doubled drive belt is used to perform the winding and twisting in one operation. The spinner's left hand guides and controls the twist coming from the wheel, while her right hand presents the correct amount of wool from the fibre supply to produce the finished yarn.*

The cover illustration is from 'The Spinstress' by George Romney and is reproduced by courtesy of the Trustees of the Iveagh Bequest, Kenwood.

SPINNING AND SPINNING WHEELS

Eliza Leadbeater

Shire Publications Ltd

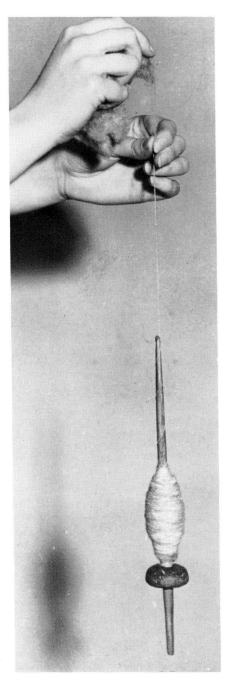

CONTENTS

Published in 2000 by Shire Publications Ltd, Cromwell House, Church Street, Princes Risborough, Buckinghamshire HP27 9AA, UK. Website: www.shirebooks.co.uk
Copyright © 1979 by Eliza Leadbeater. First published 1979; reprinted 1981, 1983, 1985, 1987, 1992, 1995 and 2000. Shire Album 43. ISBN 0 85263 469 2.

Printed in Great Britain by CIT Printing Services Ltd, Press Buildings, Merlins Bridge, Haverfordwest, Pembrokeshire SA61 1XF.

LEFT: *Spinning on a hand spindle. (Calderdale Museums Service).*

ACKNOWLEDGEMENTS
The author gratefully acknowledges the help received from Edna and Wes Blackburn; Gill Burrows for translating Diderot; Gordon Faulds for printing my photographs; John Magson of the Bankfield Museum and Halifax Piece Hall, part of the Calderdale Museums Service, which kindly photographed and permitted publication of wheels in their collection; Ann Ward and Cliffe Castle Art Gallery and Museum, which supplied the photographs on combing; Manchester Public Libraries Central Library for assistance in reproducing the Diderot prints. Permission to use photographs of wheels in their collection was kindly granted by the North American Textile Museum, North Andover, Massachusetts, USA.

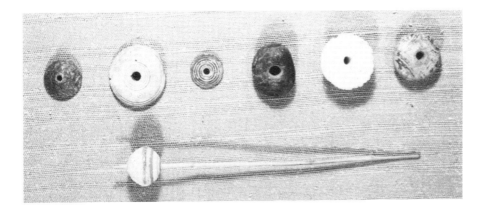

THE SPINDLE

Spinning is the drawing and twisting of fibrous materials into a continuous length, a process discovered by early man through observation and experimentation with the natural materials available to him. Although man through the ages has attempted to speed the production of thread, the principles of spinning have remained unchanged. There is a fibre supply, that is the material to be spun, a drafting area, where the fibres are drawn out to the required thickness, and a point of twist imposed by the spinning implement where the fibres are bound together. The task of the spinster is to draw out the fibres and to guide the twist.

It is a matter for conjecture how man discovered and progressed at spinning. In the beginning the twist was imposed by the rolling of the fibres between the fingers and the continuous twisted length of finger-spun yarn was stored on a stick. From this stick the primitive spindle evolved. It consisted of a slightly tapered stick with the addition of a weight known as a whorl. This whorl varied in form, but it was more often than not a disc or a ball shaped from stone, clay, bone, glass or bronze. Located either towards one end of the spindle or near its centre, the whorl functioned as a flywheel. The type of fibre spun determined the weight and proportion of the spindle and whorl. The stronger the fibre, such as flax compared with cotton, the heavier the whorl.

TOP: *A selection of ancient whorls or weights (from top left): stone, iron age 1000-900 BC; ivory, Roman 100 BC; glass, Roman, AD 300; amber, Roman, AD 300; alabaster, Byzantine, AD 600; clay, Pre-Columbian; modern African cotton spindle with painted clay whorl. (Author's collection).*

RIGHT: *Spinning consists of a fibre supply, drafting area and point of twist. Regardless of the implement used, the spinster's task is to draw out the fibres and to guide the twist.*

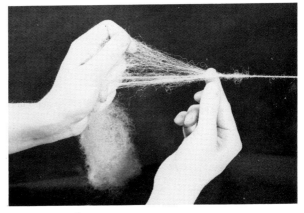

3

This primitive wheel is one step removed from a hand spindle. The spindle is mounted on a post and the whorl now functions as a pulley. The driving wheel is turned by hand and rotates the spindle. This example from Burma is made from bamboo and the rim constructed of strips. Rims were often made by a lacing of cord in place of the strips. The lowness of this wheel meant the spinner probably sat or knelt on the ground. The early charkha was probably similar in design and function. (Calderdale Museums Service).

THE GREAT WHEEL

Sometime between 500 BC and AD 750 the spindle was mechanised. This is believed to have happened in India although there is no confirmed date or agreement among historians. There existed in India a wheel known as the *charkha* which evolved from the reel used by the Chinese for unwinding raw silk from cocoons.

The spindle was now mounted horizontally between two supports, the whorl functioning as a pulley with the spindle being rotated by a belt from the whorl to a drive wheel. The charkha is thought to have reached Europe during the middle ages and was probably introduced to the British Isles from Holland in the fourteenth century.

The charkha known in India was low to the ground. In the European version the base was mounted on legs and because it was used for wool spinning it came to be known as the wool or great wheel.

OPPOSITE PAGE, TOP: An eighteenth-century illustration of a European great wheel comprising: A, its bench; b, b, 'marionettes', maidens, for support of the 'fraseaux', leathers; C, wheel; D, hub of the wheel; e, 'broche', spindle, on which the thread is wound in the shape of a cone; f, a device which stops the thread on the spindle when full; g, g, 'fraseaux' of rush folded and open to allow spindle to pass through and have free play; h, pulley over which cord from the large wheel passes; H, upright which supports the wheel, (Diderot and D'Alembert, Encyclopedie, vol. 3 1756-65. With permission of the Manchester Public Libraries, Central Library.)

4

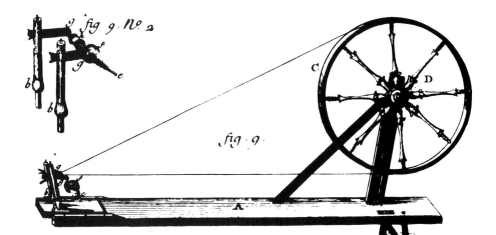

RIGHT: *The great wheel had other regional names such as the Jersey wheel. It was sometimes referred to in Scotland as the muckle wheel, in Ireland as the long wheel and in North America as the wool or walking wheel. Regardless of the style or origin of the wheel certain parts are common to all. There is a drive wheel, usually a flat rim of varying widths and constructed of wood, although a laced construction was also used. The wheel drives the spinning mechanism by means of a drive belt or cord of tightly twisted cotton or linen. The wheel is usually mounted on a post rising from a table or saddle. The table can take many forms in that it was often constructed from a rough log while others were handsomely finished and even decorated. The table or saddle is supported on two to four legs. Early manuscripts depicting the European great wheel have either two or four legs. Three-legged great wheels like this English one are similar in styling but smaller than those commonly found in North America. Rising from the table is a post on which the spindle mechanism is mounted. As in the Diderot illustration, the spindle can also be mounted between two posts or maidens. Surviving wheels throughout the British Isles more commonly have a single flat board as a post on which the spindle was mounted with leather or straw ties. A slot was cut into the post to allow room for the movement of the pulley. The pulley often contained several grooves so it could be aligned with the drive wheel. The spindle mount varies from those found in North America where the spindle assembly was usually removable. Another feature common to most great wheels was a means of adjusting the tension on the drive band. This eighteenth-century English great wheel has the additional feature of a storage tray mounted on the table. (Calderdale Museums Service).*

5

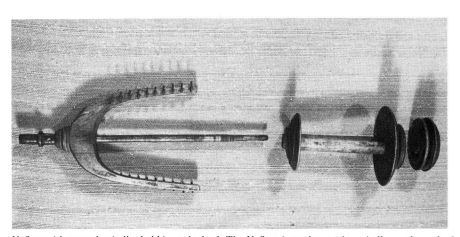

U-flyer with central spindle, bobbin and whorl. The U-flyer is made up of a spindle on the end of which is an orifice. The spun yarn passes through the orifice on to the U-shaped arms which make up the flyer. The arms are set with hooks to distribute the yarn evenly on to the bobbin. The hooks on each arm of the flyer are offset so that one set distributes yarn in the space on the bobbin left by the other set. In use the spinner works down the hooks on one side and when all have been used works back up the hooks on the other side of the flyer. The size and closeness of the hooks give an indication of the type of yarn the wheel was designed to spin, large wide-spaced hooks being for bulky yarns. Metal flyers are shaped to act as hooks and some flyers have holes and a movable hook or peg. The bobbin rotates over the flyer spindle and is driven by a pulley on its end. The diameter of the bobbin pulley is smaller than that on the whorl of the flyer spindle so that the bobbin rotates at a higher speed than the flyer, thus winding on the spun yarn (bobbin lead). The whorl serves to drive the flyer; it may have one or more grooves to give different amounts of winding and twisting for the production of different yarns. It is usually fitted with a left-hand thread on wool wheels so that the driving direction tightens it as the wool is spun. On flax wheels, where the yarn is usually spun in the opposite direction (wheel turned counter-clockwise), the whorl is often attached by a tapered fit on the spindle.

THE U-FLYER

The method of spinning was intermittent even with the introduction of the great or wool wheel as the twisting and winding on remained separate operations. But with the development of a mechanism known as a bobbin and flyer, twisting and winding were combined in one operation. This adaptation consisted of mounting a bobbin or spool on to the spindle, which was also fitted with a U-shaped arm, or flyer, to distribute the spun yarn on to the bobbin. The whorl fitted on the spindle continued to function as a pulley and another pulley was placed on one end of the bobbin so that it could also be rotated to wind up the spun yarn.

As both bobbin and flyer rotate, winding on is produced from their relative speeds of rotation. If the flyer rotates faster than the bobbin it will wrap yarn on to the slower moving bobbin *(flyer-lead)*. If the pulley is such that the bobbin rotates faster than the flyer, the bobbin will wind yarn on to itself from the flyer *(bobbin lead)*. As the bobbin becomes full the relative speeds are changed giving a different winding ratio.

To spin a consistent thread, a variable must be incorporated to compensate for this alteration. This is done by adjusting the tension on the driving band so that slip occurs keeping the rate of winding on constant. The most common and generally most successful method of producing twisting and winding is bobbin lead with both bobbin and flyer driven. In this case the diameter of the bobbin pulley is smaller than that of the flyer so the bobbin

ABOVE: *A starting length of yarn is tied on to the bobbin shaft and then taken over the hooks into the top and out of the eye of the spindle, called the orifice.*

BELOW: *In using the doubled band system a method of tensioning the band is needed so that the spinner can control the rate of winding and twisting by causing the drive belt to slip on the bobbin pulley. This is done by moving the whole assembly, termed the 'mother-of-all', along a wood screw.*

rotates faster than the flyer causing the spun yarn to be wound on to the bobbin. With this type of wheel some method of adjusting the tension on the drive belt must be provided so that a consistent yarn can be spun.

Other methods of winding are produced by introducing friction to slow either bobbin or flyer. These methods are usually not as efficient, for energy is lost in the friction of the belt.

In flyer-lead winding the flyer is driven and the bobbin is braked usually by a band over the bobbin pulley. Increased winding is produced by increased friction on the bobbin. In bobbin-lead winding the bobbin is driven and the flyer may or may not be braked. Rotation of the flyer is produced by the drag of the yarn as it is

ABOVE: *In the single-band braked bobbin system, it is not necessary to alter the tension on the driving band as the winding/twisting ratio can be altered with the bobbin brake. On this Canadian wheel the length of the drive band is made to give no slippage on the flyer pulley and the bobbin is braked by means of a band over the bobbin pulley (flyer lead over bobbin).*

TOP RIGHT: *On this wheel, winding is achieved by driving the bobbin with a single band and the pull of the spun yarn on the flyer causes it to rotate and impart the twist. The amount of twist is controlled by a brake band over the flyer orifice; in this example, this is a leather strip which is tensioned by a string passing round an adjustable peg in the maiden below the orifice. Other interesting features of this wheel are the ivory orifice and flax water pot. (Merrimack Valley Textile Museum 59.1.160).*

RIGHT: *Flyers of various sizes. (Author's collection).*

wound on the bobbin; more twist is produced by holding back the yarn causing a greater drag on the flyer and hence more rotation. Braking the flyer reduces the amount of twist in the yarn. The flyer brake is usually some device placed above the orifice bearing.

THE BOBBIN-FLYER WHEEL

Historians dispute who was the inventor of the bobbin and flyer wheel known throughout Europe and European-influenced countries. Leonardo da Vinci is often credited with designing a hand-driven spinning machine which incorporated an automatic yarn distributor. *Codex Atlantica,* a collection of his papers, contains the drawings and notes for this machine. However, there are paintings and illustrations which indicate to historians that the bobbin-flyer system evolved earlier and possibly from silk throwing.

Although the real inventor or inventors may continue to remain a mystery, it can correctly be assumed that the bobbin-flyer assembly was driven by a wheel that was turned by hand. The addition of the treadle was a later development, probably in the early seventeenth century, but the origins of this also remain undiscovered.

RIGHT AND OVER PAGE: *With treadle-operated bobbin-flyer wheels, regardless of their method of construction, origin or age, there are certain parts in common. The U-flyer and bobbin mechanism, as described in the previous chapter, is mounted usually in leathers between two posts called maidens. One of these maidens is either movable or constructed so that the bobbin-flyer can be removed for easy change of the bobbin. The maidens usually fit into a crossbar, called the mother-of-all, which is mounted on the wheel in a variety of ways. The most common mounting is a slot in the table of the horizontal wheel so that the position of the mother-of-all, and hence the tension on the drive band, can be adjusted by a wooden screw passing through the base of the mother-of-all. The wheel itself is mounted in slots in two uprights which often have stays for extra support and pegs to prevent the wheel's axle from wobbling in these slots. In some wheels only one upright is stayed — the one nearer the crank — and only one peg is used — in the opposite upright. This is because the crank upright is the one that takes the most strain directly from the crank and in a downward direction. The peg is needed in the other upright because there is an upward force on it due to the action of the crank. The wheel is rotated by this*

9

crank, being connected by a footman to a treadle. In old wheels the crank was usually bent; this served no useful purpose but was almost universally adopted. The footman was either a strip of wood or a length of cord. Many wheels were fitted with a distaff which provided a place for the fibres to be presented in a manner ready for spinning.

LEFT: *Vertical flax wheel. Although now in the USA, this wheel probably originated in Switzerland or France. There is a close-up of the metal flyer, water cup and decorative banding on the distaff on page 29. Weight was added to the small drive wheel (394 mm diameter) by banding lead in the drive belt groove. These details, and the knowledge that it was crafted from oak and satinwood, indicate a drawing-room wheel of the late eighteenth century. (Merrimack Valley Textile Museum 59.1.155).*
RIGHT: *Irish castle wheel. Unlike most vertical or upright wheels, this has the flyer assembly mounted under the drive wheel. This tripod wheel originated in the northern counties of Ireland. Of stable construction, the wheel was used primarily for spinning flax, although later for wool. On this wheel there is a wood screw to release the front maiden and remove the flyer. There is a wooden tensioning disc on the crossbar forming the mother-of-all. (Author's collection).*

EUROPEAN WHEELS

The design and shape of a wheel as well as the type of wood used are often indicators of its age and place of origin. Early wheels were crafted from oak, chestnut, sycamore, beech and various fruitwoods. Scandinavian wheels are predominantly constructed of pine and birch. During the late eighteenth century, when spinning became a fashionable pastime, wheels were made from mahogany, satinwood, boxwood and rosewood. These wheels typically had heavy staining and varnishing as well as fine or ornate turnings, which were often embellished with ivory or fancy metals such as silver or pewter.

The exact dating of any particular wheel is extremely difficult. However, a knowledge of furniture construction, woods, turnings and embellishments gives some guidance as to approximate periods. Certain characteristics of construction also assist in pinpointing a wheel to a particular region. Earlier wheels were generally, but not necessarily, coarser in construction and turning. The wheel rims tended to be thicker or deeper. The construction and incline of the table, the pivoting or construction of the treadle, the ornamentation, and the size of the orifice help in placing the origin of a wheel.

LEFT: *A woman spinning flax on a horizontal bobbin-flyer wheel. Although the wheel is fitted with a treadle the woman is turning the wheel by hand. The treadle was a later innovation to the bobbin-flyer wheel and was condemned by some because it was easy for the spinner to establish a rhythm with the foot irrespective of the requirements of the yarn being spun. The spinner welcomed the treadle as it freed both hands and speeded production. The flax is dressed on a distaff and a hand reel for skeining containing spun yarn is seen on the chair beside the spinner. (Source unknown, author's collection).*

BOTTOM LEFT: *Lidded compartment. There is no satisfactory explanation for the purpose of this compartment in the wheel's table. It is too small for spare bobbins or spinster's accessories. It is possible that a flax water pot of either tin or pewter fitted into this space.*

BELOW: *John Stewart was probably the maker of this Scottish wheel. His name is stamped in the end grain of the table. It seems remarkable that more European wheels do not bear the maker's name as they were generally made by professional craftsmen specialising in wheel or furniture construction. (Owned by D. Masterman).*

RIGHT: *Swiss/Austrian wheel. Despite its ornate turnings this wheel is capable of hard work. Its large diameter wheel (715mm) is set right down to the floor, making this a very speedy wheel. Like many similar wheels the spinner sits to the side parallel to the wheel and spins with the orifice to the right and the thread and fibre supply straight across the body. This is a comfortable position and the large base of this model makes the wheel stable, sometimes a problem with smaller wheels. The bobbin and flyer rest in wooden supports and are retained by wooden pieces kept in contact with a wood screws. These pieces also function as a flyer brake although the wheel can also be used with a doubled band. Although of no use, the turned captive rings are attractive, especially the ones on the axle of the wheel which move backwards and forwards when the wheel is in motion. (Author's collection).*

BELOW: *This attractive French flax wheel is not an efficient spinner because of the small diameter (380 mm). The triangular base is characteristic of wheels made in Normandy. It has a pewter flax cup. 'Vissant M Dep' is branded on the lower frame. This wheel is double belted. (Merrimack Valley Textile Museum 59. 1. 159).*

ABOVE: *This Finnish flax wheel is made in birch and coloured blue. The painting of birch or pine wheels appears to be a common practice. Most of the late nineteenth- and twentieth-century Finnish wheels in the author's collection are painted. The spokes are often nicely turned. The mounting of the legs in the crossbar of the treadle is another north European feature, also found on Polish and German wheels. The knob holding the treadle in place is another characteristic of these Finnish wheels. Treadles are occasionally hinged with leather and often attractively shaped. Many Scandinavian ones are decoratively carved. This wheel has a double braced upright, a feature often found in late Finnish wheels. The metal rods used as stays for the wheel supports can be used in adjusting the alignment of the wheel. (Author's collection).*

LEFT: *Double-flyer wheel. Similar in style to the other Austrian-Swiss wheel pictured, this wheel is not as stable or as well finished. It has two metal flyers designed for the spinning of flax. Flax can be spun using one hand and wheels with double flyers were designed to speed up production. Leather pads placed over the orifice act as a flyer drag and can be separately adjusted for each flyer. These wheels were made into the late nineteenth century. This wheel would have been used with a separate free standing distaff. They are more commonly found with a single flyer. (Author's collection).*

BOTTOM LEFT: *Horizontal flax wheel. This rectangular base structure, often accompanied by a heavier drive wheel and turnings, is found in Germany and parts of Italy and Switzerland. They vary from similar French wheels in that they have the treadle running parallel to the drive wheel. They also have holes rather than hooks on the flyer and work with a drag over the orifice of the flyer. (Merrimack Valley Textile Museum).*

BELOW: *Close-up of the flyer drag and hole arrangement. To distribute the spun yarn on to the bobbin, a hook is moved along the flyer arm from hole to hole.*

RIGHT: *Drawing-room wheel. This is an example of a drawing-room or boudoir wheel that became fashionable in the late eighteenth century. Ornately turned and frequently inlaid or decorated, these wheels were made of mahogany and other exotic hardwoods. The size of the wheel meant production was extremely slow, but spinning by hand was now a leisure activity taking its place alongside other needlework pursuits of the gentlewoman. (Calderdale Museums Service).*

BELOW: *Horizontal wheel. The painted trimmings, decorative turnings and the steep sloping incline of the split table are characteristics of wheels from southern Germany. Polish and Austrian wheels often have similar sloping tables. The bell-shaped distaff with water pot is original. The legs are slotted through the treadle crossbar, similar to the Finnish flax wheel, but hinged with leather. (Merrimack Valley Textile Museum).*

BOTTOM RIGHT: *Table wheel. This wheel is English and probably late eighteenth-century. The wheel, used on a table or lap, was turned by hand. Historians are uncertain of the reason for their development. Some maintain they were used for spinning fine silks or linen for lacemaking and embroidery. Others believe the wheels were used for doubling embroidery or lacemaking threads. These wheels are sometimes referred to as courting or lovers' wheels. (Calderdale Museums Service).*

15

NORTH AMERICAN WHEELS

Although America sprang from the settlements of many European nationalities, the predominant influence was British even to the household tools and wares. The great or wool wheel in the colonies was adapted from the early English one. It usually had three rather than four legs; undoubtedly this was more stable on uneven colonial floors. The spindle was usually a removable assembly mounted on a turned post. These removable mountings or heads are distinctly different from those on English wheels.

The bobbin-flyer wheel that evolved in the colonies was somewhat larger in scale than those believed to have been introduced by the Dutch into the British Isles. The American versions have come to be known as flax wheels. They are basically bobbin-lead. The early wheels were turned or crafted in oak and ash, later ones from maple and birch.

The variations on the theme of the

These photographs illustrate three types of spindle assembly common on American walking wheels.
BELOW LEFT: Minor's head. This accelerated head, patented by Amos Minor of Marcellus, New York, in 1802, increases the speed of the spindle and so aids the production of a hard high-twist yarn. These removable assemblies were extremely popular, evidently because they could be readily purchased and easily mounted on the spindle post. This no doubt accounts for the great variety of styles in walking wheels, but the similarity in accelerated heads. These usually had a stop or collar on the spindle against which the cop was formed. (Author's collection).
BELOW RIGHT: Maiden head. The spindle is held in either leathers or plaited straw or corn husks fitted to uprights similar to the maidens of the bobbin-flyer wheel. A multi-groove pulley is used so that the belt will track in the centre of the wide-rimmed wheel. (Merrimack Valley Textile Museum).
BOTTOM RIGHT: Bat head. The spindle is held in leathers fixed to a solid piece of wood from which the centre has been removed to give clearance to the pulley. Often lengths of reed or a wrapping of corn husks were fitted on to the spindle and the cop was shaped on these so it could be easily removed. (Author's collection).

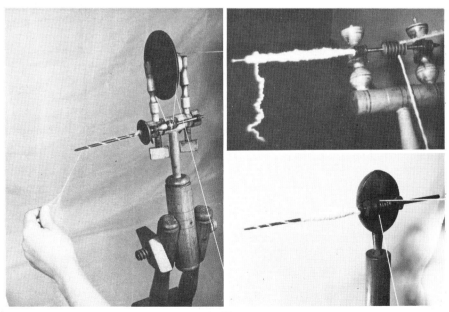

16

Ontario walking wheel. This great wheel is more commonly referred to as a walking wheel in North America because the spinner has to walk in order to perform her task. She starts close to the spindle with her right hand on the wheel and carded wool in the left. As she turns the wheel she steps back, drawing the wool out and allowing the twist from the spindle to bind the fibres together. When she has walked back as far as she can draw, the wheel is backed off (reversed) and the length of spun yarn wound on to the spindle. In colonial homes the floorboards were often considerably worn where the walking wheel was kept. This flat-rimmed wheel is 1260 mm in diameter, constructed of maple and fitted with a Minor's head. (Author's collection).

American flax wheel are quite numerous in surviving examples. There are double flyer wheels, which required the use of both hands, thereby increasing the quantity of yarn but possibly lowering the quality. There are numerous surviving examples of double treadle wheels, wheels with accelerating wheels and even pendulum sitting wool wheels.

In the early period of settlement in North America the wool supply had to be supplemented by the cultivation and spinning of flax, so both the wool wheel and the flax wheel survived side by side. The flax wheel eventually evolved into a wheel for wool production best exemplified by the Canadian Saxony or saddle wheel. This had a larger drive wheel, bobbin-flyer unit, flyer hooks, orifice and pulley-to-drive wheel ratio. These wheels were produced into the twentieth century and are among the fastest wheels for the production of wool.

TOP LEFT: *New England flax wheel. A wheel such as this has numerous names. It is referred to not only as a flax wheel, but as often as a Dutch, Low Irish or Saxony wheel. In the early seventeenth century a similar wheel found much popularity when introduced into Ireland from Holland. It is from these early wheels that many of our present-day wheels have evolved. Today's wheel has increased in diameter, and the flyer and bobbin as well as the orifice and hooks are generally designed larger to accommodate the bulkier woollen yarns craftsmen often wish to spin. (Merrimack Valley Textile Museum).*

LEFT: *Double flyer flax wheel. An attempt to speed production resulted in the development of double flyer wheels. This version was found in New York state and bears the initials 'SS' on the upper table. The top of the distaff is not original, but this one is dressed and tied with a ribbon. There are numerous ways of dressing the distaff, but in North America they were traditionally tied with either a green ribbon for the wedded or a red one for the maiden spinster. These wheels are often called gossip wheels as two spinners could share a wheel and news. (Author's collection).*

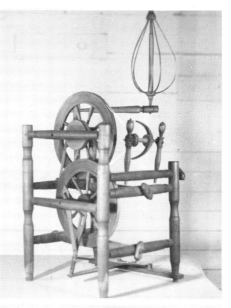

ABOVE: *Double flyer castle wheel. Once the spinner's hand was freed from turning the wheel by the introduction of the treadle in the late seventeenth century, a way was found of keeping both hands occupied. This American variation takes its name from its similarity with the Irish castle wheel, which has only one flyer. It is believed to have been made in a New England Shaker community. (Merrimack Valley Textile Museum 59.1.140).*

TOP RIGHT: *Chair wheel. The origin of these wheels is repeatedly traced to Connecticut. The style is unique to America. Apart from the chair-like frame from which it derives its name, it has several additional features including a double treadle and double wheel. The double treadle provides a smoother and more consistent rotation and means that the spinner does not have to use her hand to start the wheel. The combination of drive wheels means that with the use of smaller diameter wheels (these are about 355 mm) the rotation of the bobbin-flyer is accelerated. (Merrimack Valley Textile Museum 59.1.149).*

RIGHT: *Double treadle accelerating wheel. A variation on the chair wheel, this design speeds up production. The largest wheel drives a small solid wheel on the same axle as the smaller upper wheel and this in turn drives the bobbin and flyer. Both wheels can be tensioned as well as the mother-of-all. The presence of the lower part of the distaff is an indication that this wheel was used for flax as there is no tradition in North America of using the distaff to store prepared wool. (Author's collection).*

Industrialisation in North America was slow to oust handspinning from the home and as late as the nineteenth century innovations were being made to speed hand production or make it less laborious. This can be seen in these wheels.
ABOVE LEFT: *Hathorn's American spinner. Here is an example of Yankee ingenuity. Patented on 5th December 1871 (US Patent 121,517), this wheel was produced in Bangor, Maine, by G. H. Hathorn. As an 'American spinner' it offered a wheel with an axle at right angles to the spindle which could be either clamped to a table or mounted on a saddle as illustrated. It was as versatile as the claims made on the paper label on the side of its bed, for it combined spinner, clock reel, swift and quiller, all within an arm's reach of the spinner's chair. (Merrimack Valley Textile Museum 64.18).*
ABOVE RIGHT: *Counterbalance or pendulum wheel. This wheel enabled the spinner to sit and yet still spin on the great wheel. The spinner turns the wheel by hand and by the depression of the foot pedal the spindle moves away drawing out the wool. When its full travel has been reached the wool is backed off from the spindle by the spinner reversing the direction of the wheel and then wound up as the arm returns under the influence of the counterbalance weight and the release of the treadle. This wheel is similar in principle to the woollen mule used in industry and is really only suitable for rovings prepared by spinning machine as the amount of actual drawing out possible through the treadle action is rather small. In North America it was fairly common for households to take their own wool to a carding mill to be carded for home use. The drive from the main wheel (1290 mm diameter) is accelerated to turn the spindle. This wheel is not as attractively constructed as some. It does bear 'Patented May 22 1868 E Glendillen' on the main frame piece. (Author's collection).*
OPPOSITE PAGE, TOP LEFT: *Pendulum wheel. This is another example of a variation on a theme. This works on the same idea as the counterbalance wheel without the assistance of the weight. The wheel's diameter is 1090 mm and it was probably constructed in the same period as the other wheel. (Merrimack Valley Textile Museum).*
OPPOSITE PAGE, TOP RIGHT: *Close-up of the accelerated drive system and the tensioning arrangement for this lever-operated wheel.*

Canadian wheels. Below are three of the finest wheels for spinning wool which evolved from the flax wheel. They were all made in Canada.

BELOW LEFT: *Made in the early nineteenth century, this wheel is flat-rimmed and comes from the French region of south-west Ontario. Although it has a bobbin-flyer and is treadle-operated, there is no means of tensioning the drive belt; the bobbin is braked. The upright support of this wheel is made from one turned piece sawn in half to make the two supports. Diameter 750 mm. (Author's collection).*

BELOW CENTRE: *Made in the late nineteenth century, this is a typical Canadian wheel originating in Quebec. These French Canadian wheels were constructed of pine and painted orange, blue or red. The paint was made from buttermilk and pigment and spruced the coarse simple turnings. The tension adjustment on this wheel is an inverted U, made of metal, which passes over the mother-of-all, which rests in a slot. Tension is adjusted by rotating the mother-of-all in the slot against the friction of the metal band. The system is simple and most effective. Diameter 735 mm. (Author's collection).*

BELOW RIGHT: *Wool spinning reached its heights in this Canadian double treadle wheel. It is one of the largest diameter (760 mm) treadle wheels. Constructed of unpainted pine and maple, the turnings and general finish are more elaborate than on the Quebec wheel. The double treadle and large wheel mean more power is available. The footmen are of sturdy wire. Tensioning is similar to the previous wheel, but there is no handle on the mother-of-all. The wheel is extremely fast and the larger bobbin-flyer makes it most suitable for wool. Constructed in the late nineteenth or early twentieth century, this wheel exemplifies all that is ideal in a wheel. Another variation was a similar wheel fitted with a single treadle constructed from cast iron. Diameter 760mm. (Author's collection).*

Shears were used by a variety of wool workers, from the shepherd for shearing the sheep to the burler, who made good the defects in the woven cloth, and the cloth dresser or cropper, who cut the nap of the cloth to a uniform length. (Calderdale Museums Service).

WOOL TOOLS

The tools for the preparation of fibres before spinning are as interesting as the wheels themselves. However, fewer have survived, undoubtedly because a wheel to any generation is a nostalgic relic of a bygone age. Fortunately, for this reason there has always been a corner in a room or a loft to save a wheel. Fewer tools are in evidence, but archaeological findings show that early civilisations were versed in the importance of sound fibre preparation for the production of good quality threads and therefore different tools were developed for the various fibres.

In the British Isles there is a rich tradition in producing wool. Wool is the fibrous coat of the sheep; other fibre-bearing animals produce either hair or fur. In ancient times sheep moulted, so their wool was originally plucked by bronze-age shepherds. This practice, known as rooing, is still employed today on the primitive descendants of these early breeds.

Shearing is the usual means of removing the sheep's coat or fleece. It is a strenuous skill as the wool must be removed without injuring the animal. Shears first appeared during the iron age and have remained virtually unchanged. They consist of two metal knives joined by a spring. Hand-shears have now given way to mechanical blades, similar to the hairdressing shears most of us are familiar with and powered by hand, steam, petrol or electricity. The process has now been speeded up.

Next the wool was sorted into qualities, that is degrees of fineness, and then scoured. The scoured fibres were often 'wuzzed', a method of removing excess water to hasten drying. Wool must next be disentangled. In prehistoric Europe this was done by beating the wool with a length of gut strung on a bow. The preparation methods of combing and carding were practised by medieval times.

Carding is a means of preparation in which the fibres are brushed between two paddles of hooked teeth. Dried teasels (*Dipsacus fullonum*) set in a cross are

22

believed to have been first used. These teasel crosses, known as strikers, have been used for raising the nap on cloth during finishing. It is not until the thirteenth century that there is evidence that teasels or thorns were replaced by wire teeth. These wire teeth were individually cut, bent and set into a leather backing. The making of the wire teeth was a laborious task until the end of the eighteenth century when a machine was invented that cut, bent and set the teeth.

Combing is another method of disentangling the fibres. It is a process by which the short fibres are removed and the long fibres are arranged parallel so that the resulting spun yarn is smooth in appearance. The combs pictured in early manuscripts and prints vary but those that had evolved by the nineteenth century were T-shaped handles with two to eight rows of tapered metal teeth. Used in pairs, each comb weighed an average of 4 kilograms (9 pounds). The craft of combing required both skill and strength.

Following shearing, wool was sorted into qualities, washed, rinsed, then hung on a frame to dry, before further sorting and the task of untangling the fibres. Beating (fig. 5) was a step in the process of opening the fibres. The wool was beaten with sticks on a screen made from rope to release dirt and vegetable matter. Beating was followed by picking, which further teased and opened the fibres. Finally the wool was ready for carding and either a carding horse (fig. 6) or handcards (fig. 7) were used. Industrialisation has hastened and mechanised these tasks. The picture shows beating as it was carried out in eighteenth-century France. Today handspinners follow similar stages in the preparation of wool. (Diderot and D'Alembert. Encyclopedie, vol. 3, 1756-65. With permission of the Manchester Public Libraries, Central Library.)

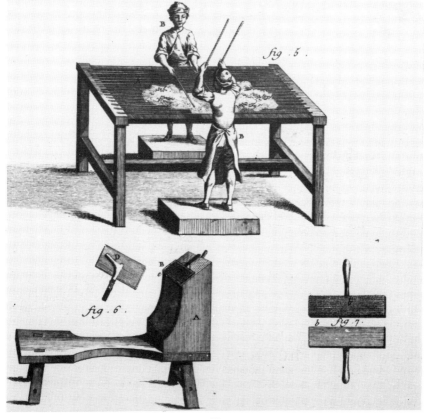

ABOVE: *This sketch represents the card-maker's shop. One worker (fig. 1) is using a fork to prick a skin stretched on the 'panteur'. After the skin has been stretched and pricked, a worker (fig. 2) sets the pins. Another worker (fig. 3) has the task of preparing the wooden paddle on which the skin with teeth is mounted. The making of card clothing by hand continued until 1797 when a machine was invented by an American, Amos Whittemore, which could individually cut, bend and set the hundreds of wire teeth into the leather backing. (Diderot and D'Alembert, Encyclopedie, vol. 2, 1756-65. With permission of the Manchester Public Libraries, Central Library.)*

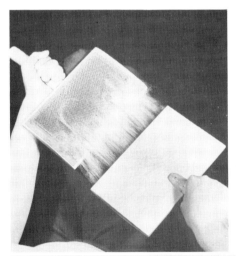

LEFT: *Carding, the preparation necessary for spinning a woollen yarn, involves the opening and straightening of the fibres by brushing them between two specially designed paddles. By this method the fibres are fluffed and arranged to lie in one direction; they are then rolled into a tube shape called a rolag. When spun the fibres lie perpendicular to the direction of the twist and the yarn produced is spongy in texture owing to the trapped air.*

BELOW: *Wool combs, although widely used, varied considerably in design from a single row of broitches to an arrangement of several rows gradated in size. (Merrimack Valley Textile Museum).*

ABOVE AND NEXT PAGE: *Combing as a craft was destroyed in the nineteenth century by the introduction of machinery. The main items in the comber's workshop were a vertical post, an iron pad, a stove, an oil can and two pairs of combs. The stove or pot burned either coal or charcoal and was used to heat the combs; this helped to soften the lanolin and make the wool easier to work. The stove accommodated four combs and was often referred to as a 'pot of four'. The combs had three to eight rows of tapered steel teeth known as broitches. A comb was mounted on the iron pad fixed to the post and then the scoured wool was pulled by hand on to the broitches, a process sometimes referred to as 'donning on'. The filled comb was mounted with its teeth parallel to the ground and a second heated comb was now swung with a vertical motion to draw the wool from the static comb. This action of 'jigging' was repeated until the long fibres were removed. The newly filled comb was either transferred to the post or the wool itself was transferred to the original comb. During the entire process*

25

the combs were kept warm by returning them to the pot. Once jigged, the wool was then drawn off into lengths of about 2 yards (1.8 metres) called 'sleevers', which were temporarily stored as a ball. The sleevers were then broken into lengths of 8 to 10 inches (200 to 250mm), oiled and jigged again. Finally the wool was drawn off the filled comb through a horn disc, called a 'diz', which served to check the consistency of the sleevers. Before machinery replaced the comber he could earn about twenty shillings per week with the pay varying from 2½d to 2s 4d per pound. (Cliffe Castle Museum and Art Gallery, Keighley, West Yorkshire).

FLAX TOOLS

Flax *(Linum usitatissimum)* is believed to have been discovered in prehistoric times and has been widely cultivated to the present day. The seeds are sown very closely to prevent the plant branching and the plant is ready to harvest when two thirds of the stem from the root upwards turn yellow. It is then pulled by hand to preserve the full length of the fibres including the root. After drying, the heads of the plants are drawn through a coarse comb called a rippler to remove the seed capsules. The flax is then retted.

Retting is a process of fermentation by which air and moisture decompose the adhesive substances that bind the fibres in bundles about the woody inner core of the plant's stem. The flax tools are for breaking up and removing this woody inner core and combing and arranging the fibres in preparation for spinning.

After retting, the plant's stems were again dried and then beaten with a wooden mallet to remove the useless woody core or boon. The mallet was replaced in the fourteenth century by a break or brake. The flax break consisted of a number of wooden knives mounted in a frame which, when banged together, broke up the inner core leaving the outer bundles of fibres unharmed. The flax was then beaten with a wooden knife against a wooden, vertically mounted board. This was known as scutching or swingling and

LEFT: *This wheel with distaff is typical of those used for the spinning of flax. (Merrimack Valley Textile Museum).*
RIGHT: *This eighteenth-century wheel was designed with a large bobbin-flyer (430 mm length. 280 mm span) for spinning tow. The diameter of the orifice is 7 mm. There are wire hooks on one arm of the flyer to guide the spun yarn. (Merrimack Valley Textile Museum 59.1.139).*

further assisted in removing the remaining bits of boon left after breaking.

The fibres were then ready for the final operation, hackling. Hackling was a method of combing the fibres to separate them further and arrange them parallel. This was achieved by drawing the fibres until they were straightened and the short bits removed through a series of combs called hackles or heckles. The hackles consisted of rows of pointed teeth set in a board. The first hackle was called a ruffler; it has the coarsest setting of the teeth. The process of drawing and straightening was done to both ends of the bundle through to the middle. The process was repeated through a series of hackles, each progressively more finely toothed. The short bits of fibre that remain in the

hackle were known as tow. Tow was used for making ropes. The long, fine, parallel groups of fibres that were combed through the hackle are known as line. Line was stored in bundles called queues or stricks. These were the fibres that the spinster arranged on her distaff and spun into linen yarn.

Distaffs varied considerably. They were implements on which to arrange the fibres so that the spinner had a constant fibre supply. Many flax wheels have a hole on the table or saddle to accommodate an arm or tapered stick. If a wheel does not have a hole for a distaff this does not mean that it was not used for flax, because often the fibres were arranged on a free standing distaff. These resembled a length of stick, often tapered or decoratively

Although the workers in this eighteenth-century French print are processing hemp, flax was prepared in a similar fashion. Fig. 1. Men are busy placing the bundles of fibres into the 'routoir' or retting pond. The bundles are covered with planks which are then loaded with stones to keep the bundles under water and prevent them from floating up. Fig. 2. Seed capsules being removed on a ripple. Fig. 3. The shed where the fibres are dried by spreading them on poles above a fire of chenevote or boon. Fig. 4. A woman stripping the stems to see if the fibres are ready for the breaking and beating. Fig. 5. The breaker or dresser. Figs. 6,7,8. The beaters or scutchers. Diderot and D'Alembert, Encyclopedie, vol. 1, 1756-65. With permission of the Manchester Public Libraries, Central Library).

turned, set into a small stool. Distaffs were not only tapered but also often lantern-shaped, many being fashioned from branches. Others were prong-shaped or comb-like in construction.

Another useful accessory to the flax spinner was her cup or water pot. Those that have survived are of pewter or carved wood. They were fastened or hung on the wheel so that the spinster could moisten her fingers, which was necessary for spinning a smooth linen yarn.

Water pots took a variety of forms and were either hung from the wheel or formed an integral part of it. This is an example of a hanging pot on an early New England wheel. (Merrimack Valley Textile Museum).

28

ABOVE: *Distaffs took many forms and were designed to be a removable part of a horizontal wheel. The shape of the upper part varied considerably; in its most primitive form it was a branch or a basket or a basket formed from a branch. Others were lantern or bell-shaped, while in Russia and parts of northern and eastern Europe the distaff resembled a comb. (Merrimack Valley Textile Museum).*

TOP RIGHT: *Vertical flax wheels often had long tapered or decoratively turned distaffs, particularly in regions where the hackled line was simply fastened to the rock (another word for distaff) rather than arranged or dressed. A water cup is also fitted to this distaff, which is seen in its storage position. (Merrimack Valley Textile Museum).*

RIGHT: *This vertical wheel has its water cup attached to the maiden. It has several features worth noting. The distaff is banded with silver and the groove of the wheel weighted with lead. The arms of this flyer are made from metal. (Merrimack Valley Textile Museum 59.1.155).*

29

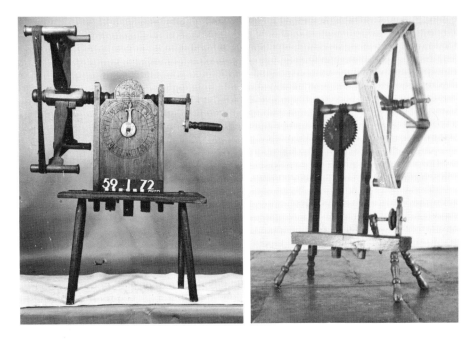

LEFT: *The year '1749' and 'Daniel Abbot' are carved above the clock face of this rotary type skeiner. When a clock-like face was used to indicate the number of rounds, the skeiner was termed a clock-reel. (Merrimack Valley Textile Museum).*
RIGHT: *This click-reel from the New England region of the USA has a 2 yard (1.8 metre) circumference and signals forty rounds. (Author's collection).*

ACCESSORIES

There were other accessories used by the spinner. Some wheels incorporate a rack on which to store extra bobbins. Bobbin racks, used to hold two or more bobbins, were also useful when doubling yarn.

The yarn, once spun, had to be removed from the bobbin. The reel was developed for this tedious task of measuring and skeining the spun yarn. It consisted of a stick with two short arms at each end, similar to the capital letter I. A variation was developed where one of the arms turned at a right angle to the other; this doubled the length of the skein. This variation was known as a cross-reel or niddy-noddy. The circumference of the skeins varied with locality. Because it was used for measuring and the error that could accumulate over four sections was considerable the niddy-noddy was replaced by a rotary type of winder.

This rotary winder, also hand-operated, consisted of four or six arms and had a geared cog to count the number of rounds. The rounds were indicated either by a hand on a clock-like face or by a click or loud snap produced by twanging a flexible piece of wood with a peg set in the counting cog. The yarn was now ready to be washed, dyed and wound into balls for use by the weaver, lacemaker or knitter.

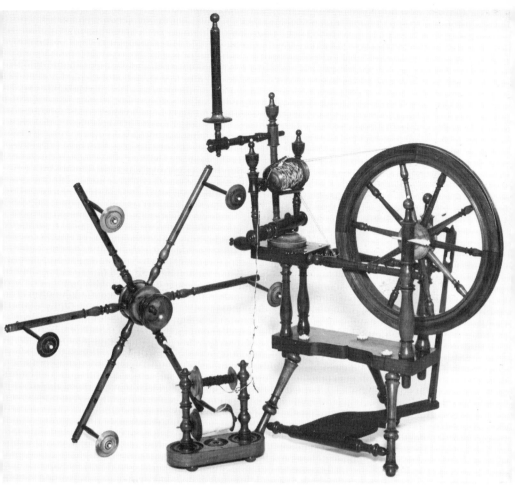

ABOVE: *This is a traditional Scandinavian-style wheel with a flat table and horizontal stays which screw through the wheel supports so that the alignment of the wheel can be adjusted. The wheel is fitted with a distaff and has a companion bobbin rack and skeiner. (Calderdale Museums Service).*

RIGHT: *The niddy-noddy is a simple form of a reel. This one is an eighteenth-century Pennsylvania-German courting gift. (Merrimack Valley Textile Museum).*

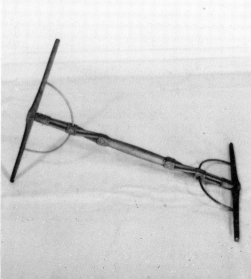

FURTHER READING

(Several of these recommended books* are out of print, but available through libraries.)

Baines, Patricia. *Spinning Wheels, Spinners and Spinning*. Batsford, 1977.
Burnham, H. B. and D. K. *Keep Me Warm One Night*. University of Toronto, 1972.
Channing, M. L. *Textile Tools of Colonial Homes*. 1969.
Crowfoot, G. M., and Roth, H. Ling. *Hand Spinning and Wool Combing*. R. Bean Publications, reprinted 1974.
Cummer, Joan Whittaker. *A Book of Spinning Wheels*. Peter Randall Publisher, 1993.
Davenport, Elsie. * *Your Handspinning*. Select Books, 1964.
Forbes, R. J. *Studies in Ancient Technology*. William S. Heinman, 1964.
Hochberg, Bette. *Handspindles*. Straw into Gold Distributors, 1977.
Leadbeater, Eliza. *Handspinning*. Macmillan/Select Books, 1976.
Pennington, D., and Taylor, M. *Pictorial Guide to American Spinning Wheels*. Shaker Press, 1975.
Teal, Peter. *Hand Woolcombing and Spinning*. Blandford Press, 1976.
Thompson, G.B. *Spinning Wheels (John Horner Collection)*. Ulster Museum, 1964.

PLACES TO VISIT

Museum displays may be altered and readers are advised to telephone before visiting to check that relevant items are on show, as well as to find out the opening times.

American Museum in Britain, Claverton Manor, Bath BA2 7BD. Telephone: 01225 460503.
Bankfield Museum, Boothtown Road, Halifax, West Yorkshire HX3 6HG. Telephone: 01422 354823 or 352334.
Bradford Industrial Museum, Moorside Road, Eccleshill, Bradford, West Yorkshire BD2 3HP. Telephone: 01274 631756.
Calderdale Industrial Museum, Central Works, Square Road, Halifax, West Yorkshire HX1 0QG. Telephone: 01422 358087. (By appointment only.)
Cliffe Castle Museum, Spring Gardens Lane, Keighley, West Yorkshire BD20 6LH. Telephone: 01535 618230 or 618231.
Cregneash Village Folk Museum, Cregneash, Isle of Man. Telephone: 01624 675522.
Helmshore Textile Museums, Holcombe Road, Helmshore, Rossendale, Lancashire BB4 4NP. Telephone: 01706 226459.
Lewis Museum of Textile Machinery, Exchange Street, Blackburn, Lancashire. Telephone: 01254 667130.
Museum of Local Crafts and Industries, Towneley Hall, Towneley Park, Burnley, Lancashire BB11 3RQ. Telephone: 01282 424213.
Museum of Welsh Life, St Fagans, Cardiff CF5 6XB. Telephone: 01222 573500. Website: www.nmgw.ac.uk
Quarry Bank Mill, Styal, Cheshire SK9 4LA. Telephone: 01625 527468. Website: www.rmplc.co.uk/orgs/quarrybankmill
Royal Museum of Scotland, Chambers Street, Edinburgh EH1 1JF. Telephone: 0131 225 7534. Website: www.nms.ac.uk
Snowshill Manor, near Broadway, Worcestershire WR12 7JU. Telephone: 01386 852410. Website: www.ntrustsevern.org.uk
Stewartry Museum, St Mary Street, Kirkcudbright DG6 4AQ. Telephone: 01557 331643.
Ulster Folk and Transport Museum, Cultra, Holywood, County Down BT18 0EU. Telephone: 01232 428428. Website: www.nidex.com/uftm
Ulster Museum, Botanic Gardens, Belfast BT9 5AB. Telephone: 01232 383000.
York Castle Museum, Eye of York, York YO1 9RY. Telephone: 01904 613161. Website: www.york.gov.uk/heritage/museums/castle